Jesus Reflects

Monologues And Children's
Lessons For Advent
And Christmas

Edward G. Hunter

CSS Publishing Company, Inc.
Lima, Ohio

JESUS REFLECTS

Copyright © 1994 by
The CSS Publishing Company, Inc.
Lima, Ohio

Scripture quotations are from the *New Revised Standard Version of the Bible,* copyright 1989 by the Division of Christian Education of the National Council of the Churches of Christ in the USA. Used by permission.

Library of Congress Cataloging-in-Publication Data

Hunter, Edward G., 1924-
    Jesus reflects : monologues and children's sermons for Advent and Christmas / Edward G. Hunter.
    p.   cm.
    ISBN 0-7880-0110-8
    1. Advent sermons. 2. Christmas sermons. 3. Children's sermons. 4. Sermons, American. I. Title.
BV40.H86   1994
252'.53—dc20   94-6761
                                          CIP

This book is available in the following formats, listed by ISBN:
0-7880-0110-8 Book
0-7880-0111-6 IBM (3 1/2 and 5 1/4) computer disk
0-7880-0112-4 IBM book and disk package
0-7880-0113-2 Macintosh computer disk
0-7880-0114-0 Macintosh book and disk package

PRINTED IN U.S.A.

*With love to
my wife, Lavine, and
our three children,
Sydne, Craig, and Blake*

Table of Contents

Introduction

These monologues and children's sermons are primarily for worship services during the Advent/Christmas season, whether morning or evening. But, they are not limited to that. The monologues in particular can be used for devotional readings, for meetings, church school assemblies (or individual classes), women's meetings, men's meetings, youth gatherings, and so forth.

You will find that it makes the listeners feel as if "they are there." It puts them "in the picture," so to speak.

I have used several of these in different gatherings, and in worship services on Sunday morning and evening, and they have been well received.

Laypersons can be very effective as readers, so long as they have a dramatic sense and a clear, resonant voice.

Some of these (such as Joseph, Mary, Melchior, the Innkeeper) can be used in evening sessions, preferably in the sanctuary, with the lights dimmed (or completely out) and the only light on the pulpit or speaker's rostrum (for the reader). A quiet, unobstrusive background of seasonal music is also effective. It will make a memorable worship service for the Christmas season.

Be innovative. Make the service "come alive" with the reading, music, and liturgy (minimal). Make an announcement at the beginning that you want to place the audience in the original setting, as nearly as possible. They are to let their imaginations take flight!

I would be so bold as to say you will be pleasantly surprised with the results!

Thanksgiving Sunday/Day
A Dramatic Monologue
Suggested Scripture: Psalm 107:1-8

A Pilgrim Recounts

My name is Silas. I am one of the original 103 pilgrims who sailed on the *Mayflower* from England to America, in the year of our Lord, 1620. I have now been in the new world for ten years, and each year since we first arrived we have celebrated three days of Thanksgiving in November. It is on that first day of thanksgiving, November 29, 1630, that I wish to recount some of the trials and tribulations we underwent in our journey to this new land.

I need to tell you why we made the 10-week journey across the vast and turbulent ocean. To do that, I must recount some of our history as Separatists (the title given to us many years ago in England). When Henry the Eighth broke with the Roman Catholic Church in 1531, shortly after the Protestant Reformation in Germany, many thought he had made a clean break with the Catholic Church. But, many of us did not. We wanted to go further than the 39 Articles of Religion formulated by the Anglican Church. We wanted to ordain our own clergy, have our own church government, and worship God according to the dictates of our conscience. The Church of England, in 1603, under King James the First, began to persecute our small band for what they called our "radical thinking." They would not allow us to have our own worship services, nor our own ministers and, if we continued to do so, we would be imprisoned. Indeed, many of us were. Our religious freedom was basically denied, so we sought another country in which to practice our faith. At first we set up a colony in Holland, but the language became such a barrier that we stayed but a short time. We then determined to sail to the new world.

I was a part of the congregation from Scrooby, England, that made up the first group of pilgrims that sailed to America. We left Delft Haven in 1620. I still remember the resonant voice of our pastor, John Robinson, as he led 103 of us from the church to the harbor. He read from the Book of Genesis, the 12th chapter, verses one through three. I can still hear his magnificent voice as he proclaimed aloud: "Get thee out of thy country, and from thy kindred — unto a land that I will show thee: And I will make of thee a great nation, and in thee shall all the families of the earth be blessed." We believed, somehow, it would be so!

The ten-week journey on our ship, the *Mayflower*, was much more difficult than we imagined it would be. We would have horrendous storms at sea, with all of us deathly ill. We were not seamen; we were craftsmen, artisans, carpenters, printers and clothmakers. But, we must have been sturdy souls, for we lost but one of our group to death during that arduous journey.

We finally arrived at what is now called Cape Cod Bay on November 11, 1620. It was a bitter cold day, and it was snowing hard. We dropped anchor for the first time since we left England. Several men (including myself) rowed to shore and scouted around. The terrain was frozen and so rocky we knew we would be unable to construct any habitation and the land was too rocky for farming. One of our group found a buried sack of Indian corn which we carried back to the *Mayflower*. Providence be praised! It would be our basic food for the entire next year! Our grain which we brought from England proved unfruitful in American soil.

We stayed on board the *Mayflower* for another month, scouting out other habitations, but found none suitable. On December 16 we anchored at what would become known later as Plymouth Bay, and on December 21 disembarked on the land where we have remained for some ten years now. In the spring, as I mentioned, we planted our seed from England and it did not harvest. Someone mentioned the Indian corn we had found at Cape Cod Bay, so we planted it the next spring. It harvested to a bumper crop, and kept us from starvation! Who can understand the ways of the Almighty in allowing us to find that grain in a deserted Indian village?

We had to pool all of our resources that first year. None of us could survive alone. We ate in communal gatherings; we shared what animals and fowl we killed; we shared what grain we had; we made clothing for one another; we even shared shoes.

That first winter was the hardest. We lost almost half of our entire group. Forty-two perished from illness, cold, and hard labor, including my beloved wife Miriam. Then it was only my 16-year-old son, Silas, Jr., and myself.

I must tell you about our first Thanksgiving! Not long after we arrived in Plymouth an Indian by the name of Squanto suddenly appeared out of the woods and spoke to us in good English! He and his tribe had been taught by a group of navy men who had stayed with them several years before. Squanto introduced us to Massassoit, chief of his tribe, and we immediately drew up a peace agreement to ensure tranquility among both groups. It has lasted these ten years without any hostility between us, and there is good reason to believe it will last for years to come.

After our first year in America we celebrated our first Thanksgiving the next autumn. We invited Massassoit and 90 other American Indians to our first Thanksgiving. You might be interested to know what our Thanksgiving meal consisted of: Massassoit brought six deer for the occasion. We killed and roasted a good supply of wild turkey, geese, duck and fish. We also had journey cake, corn meal bread with nuts, and succotash. Dessert was pumpkin pie cooked in maple fat. There was more than enough food for the three days of celebration. By the way, our Thanksgiving was not primarily feasting; it was a time of grateful prayer and the singing of many hymns and psalms. We will be forever grateful to the Almighty for sparing so many of us in those early days.

It was William Bradford, our first governor, who made the official proclamation of Thanksgiving three years after we arrived, an observance we would honor each year. It read: "Inasmuch as the Great Father has given us this year an abundant harvest of Indian corn, wheat, peas, beans, squashes, and garden vegetables, and has made the forest to abound with game and the sea with fishes and clams, and inasmuch as he has protected us from the ravages of the savages, has spared us from pestilence and disease, has granted us freedom to worship God according to the dictates of our own conscience; Now, I, your magistrate, do proclaim that all ye pilgrims, with your wives and ye little ones, do gather at ye meethouse on ye hill, between the hours of 9 and 12 in the daytime, on Thursday, November ye 29th of the year of our Lord one thousand six hundred and twenty-three, and the third year since ye pilgrims landed on ye Plymouth Rock, there to listen to ye pastor and render thanksgiving to ye Almighty God for all his blessings."

When the *Mayflower* crew left to return the next spring after we arrived, each of us was asked if he or she wanted to return to England. None of us wished to return. We had found what we had searched for. A land where we could be free to worship as we pleased, where we were free to govern ourselves, and free to live in peace and freedom — not only for ourselves but for succeeding generations.

Thanksgiving is really a daily celebration for us, for we all remember the hardship of those early years. We wish never to take the blessings of Almighty God for granted, and trust that succeeding generations will not do so either.

Children's Sermon
Thanksgiving Sunday

Five Kernels
Of Corn

Object: Five kernels of corn

Today is Thanksgiving Sunday. Why do we have a day for Thanksgiving? In order to give God thanks for the many good things we enjoy: such as our home, our church, our school, our parents, our friends, our food, our clothing.

The early Pilgrims were very thankful to God when they first arrived in America in 1620. They were thankful for a safe voyage over the Atlantic Ocean. The voyage took them ten weeks. They experienced many bad storms at sea. They had to ration their food. Does anyone know what "ration" means? It means that everyone had just so much to eat and no more for there was not a lot of food. They lost one of their group in death out of 103. The first year they were in America 42, of the 102 who were left, died. Almost half their group!

They found that the grain they had brought over from England would not grow in American soil, so they nearly starved their first year here. Fortunately they found a sack of Indian corn in a deserted Indian village near Plymouth Rock. Each family was given five grains of corn to plant the next spring, and it turned out to be enough corn for everyone when they pooled it altogether!

In November of 1621 they celebrated their first Thanksgiving in America. Now they had plenty of food, including corn, wild turkey, deer meat, vegetables, and pumpkin pie!

Those who prepared the meal put five kernels of corn on each plate to remind them of their first hard year, and how

God had supplied their need by letting them find the Indian corn. For many years after that, at their Thanksgiving feast, they would put five kernels of corn on each plate.

Perhaps we need to put something on our plates to remind us of the good things we enjoy and many times take for granted. Maybe it could be some small amount of money to remind us that God supplies our monetary needs, with which we buy our clothing and our food, and even the house we live in. Maybe it could be a bottle of medicine to remind us that we have hospitals and doctors and nurses and medicine to help us when we get sick. Maybe it should be a picture of our family, to remind us of the wonderful parents and brothers and sisters we have.

You know what I would put on my plate? A picture of Jesus, to remind me of the greatest gift God has given us — his Son. Each of you would have something special on your plate, something you are truly grateful for, I'm sure.

Let us not just thank God one day of the year, such as Thanksgiving. Let us thank God every day for his many blessings to us. As the Apostle Paul tells us: "In *everything* give thanks."

A Shepherd Returns

An elderly shepherd, one of the original group who heard the angelic announcement that first Christmas Eve, speaks to his son, also a shepherd, outside the cave where Jesus was born:

"My son, here in this humble stable is his birthplace. I remember the night as if it were yesterday — though it is now 50, nay, 51 years ago! I have come here each year at this time. Something draws me here. Had you seen and heard what I did, you, too, would be drawn here. Look! Others have come now. Every year there are a few more. They come in spite of the fact that it is dangerous to be here. If I had the gift of a prophet I would say that, someday, hundreds, nay thousands, will come to this place!"

The son speaks: "But, my father, you know that Nero has determined to rid the world of all those who call themselves Christian. The Jewish authorities have joined him in persecuting those who are 'Followers of the Way.' Even now, wherever they are found, they are tortured until they either deny him, or become a human torch in Nero's garden. They are even torn to pieces by wild beasts in the circuses! How can they survive?"

"I am only a humble shepherd, my son, the son and the grandson of a shepherd, but I believe the Followers of the Way will continue to grow in spite of persecution and death. The Roman Empire will crumble into dust before they are eliminated. Everyone underestimates the power of the One we follow. You, yourself, are but a recent member of the Christian

15

sect. I have followed him most of my life. I have seen men and women die rather than deny him. Faith such as that cannot be killed. It is stronger than death! If I should have to give my life, it is a small price to pay for allegiance to him. There is no meaning to life apart from him.

"But, I promised to tell you of the events of that night. There are not many of the original group left. One by one they pass from this life. But, I can see it yet! It makes my heart pound to think again of that night!

"I ask myself time and again, why us, a group of lowly shepherds? Why not Augustus Caesar, or Caiaphas, or even Pilate? Who can understand the ways of the Almighty? But, it was to *us* he appeared! That heavenly Messenger! I can see him yet as plainly as I see you, enveloped in heavenly light. I was not as old as you. We fell as dead men. We were terrified! At first I thought it was a dream, perhaps an hallucination. But we all saw the same thing. We heard the same voice. Heard the same heavenly chorus. I have never heard such voices! We could not deny what our eyes had seen and our ears had heard!

"I remember Luke, the physician, seeking out several of us a few years later to get an eye-witness account of what took place that night. We all agreed that what he wrote in his gospel said it quite accurately. I have memorized his words, so beautifully, so accurately written: 'In that region there were shepherds living in the fields, keeping watch over their flock by night. Then an angel of the Lord stood before them, and the glory of the Lord shone around them, and they were terrified. But the angel said unto them, "Do not be afraid; for see — I am bringing you good news of great joy for all the people: to you is born this day in the city of David a Savior, who is the Messiah, the Lord. This will be a sign for you: you will find a child wrapped in bands of cloth, and lying in a manger." '

"That is just the way it happened. My brothers and I still could not believe what we had seen and heard. We thought about it. We discussed it. Were our minds deceiving us? We were too frightened to go, and too filled with wonder to stay. We *had* to go into the city in that early morning hour. And find, who? The *Messiah?* The long-awaited Deliverer from God? No, no, it could not be! We had waited for centuries. We had prayed earnestly for his coming, but he had not come. Why, in the name of all that's holy, would his birth be announced to *us?*

"Nevertheless, we made our way over the hillside to Bethlehem. We roamed each and every street, looking for signs: the stable, the manger, the newborn babe. It was my youngest brother, Amos, who found him. He came running to us, breathless. He told us where he had found him, and we came, here, to this very spot. In the back of this cave there was a young woman with her newborn babe. You wonder how we knew? I cannot tell you, but *we knew!* We spoke not a word at first. His mother was sound asleep, and his father only looked at us. Finally the father spoke, asking us why we had come. One of the group spoke to him briefly, explaining the angelic visitation. He seemed to understand, and didn't ask for any explanation.

"We stayed. I don't know how long. I think only a brief time. Though it seemed as if time stood still. We finally left, filled with wonder. I can remember contradictory thoughts racing through my mind: How could it be? The Promised One of God, the Messiah, born in a *stable?* To two young peasants? He could not come in this manner! But, I could not deny the angelic visitation, his words, the spirit of wonder to it all. It was beyond our comprehension. Far beyond our comprehension.

"I kept close watch on that child, privately. I found out where he and his family lived in Nazareth. I inquired about his father, Joseph, the carpenter. Once I went into his shop. I asked about the young Jesus. He looked at me with a puzzled expression. 'Strange that you should ask about Jesus, though many do. He is not here. Probably somewhere in the countryside, or even at the synagogue with the rabbis, one of his favorite places. I still don't understand the lad. He lives in another world. He speaks a language I nor his mother understand. But given his unusual birth, and I won't go into that, it could not be otherwise.' We talked at some length, and I explained to him that I was one of the shepherds who came into the cave that night. He was astounded and said we had to talk! He confided things to me about the young Jesus. He seemed to know that his Son was headed toward *danger!* Jesus was too vocal in his criticism of the religious authorities. Joseph feared for his son's life at times, but felt he was helpless to do anything about it. He had promised God a long time ago that he would not interfere in his life. He belonged to God. God had told him, through prayer, and in dreams, that he would take care of the lad. What more could he do than leave him in God's hands?''

The elderly shepherd continues: ''I followed his life closely. I heard him speak a number of times on the hillside, or in the temple courtyard. I saw him heal, even a man blind from birth. He healed the sick before my very eyes. He cast out demons from the insane. It was said that he even raised a young girl who had died, yes, *died,* to life! Something I myself did not see. But have no reason whatever to doubt.

''I knew he was courting danger. The Jewish elders, especially the Pharisees, were beside themselves with anger. He was too dangerous to live! I thought at the time it was an idle threat, but, as you know, it turned out to be true.

''Aha! but I have not told you the most important thing for me personally! *I talked to him* one time! He was on the road from Jerusalem to Galilee. I came up beside him, and asked if I might not walk with him a little way. He said, 'Of course.' I finally gathered enough courage to tell him I was one of the shepherds who heard the announcement of his birth on the hillside. He stopped dead in his tracks. He turned and looked me fully in the eyes. 'I have never talked to one of the eye-witnesses,' he said. 'I have only heard the story told to me by my mother and father. Why have you not spoken sooner?' I was embarrassed, but he wanted to put me at ease. I spoke fully of that night, of our visit to the cave. I told him of my interest in his ministry and my admiration for all he was doing. He smiled and said, 'Don't be merely a spectator, be a participant.' I told him I already was.

"I remember the day he rode into Jerusalem on the donkey. The cleansing of the temple. The betrayal in the garden. The trial before Pilate. And then his horrible crucifixion. I was numb throughout the whole proceedings.

"Oh, but I remember far more the morning we received the news of his — yes — his resurrection! It went through the area like wildfire. Most would not believe. Many are still not convinced. But he *appeared* to more than 500 in his resurrection body! I was among them. How can we deny what our eyes have seen?

"Memories. Memories. My mind is flooded with haunting memories.

"Look, my son, the sun is rising! So much like the day he was born! I wonder every year if we are near the time when he will rule the hearts of all men and women. But now, with the persecution by Nero, will the Way survive? Yes, somehow, someway, I believe it will. *Can anyone defeat God?*

"Would God send such a precious Light into the world if he did not believe that all men would follow it . . . *someday?*"

The
Christmas Gift

Object: A wrapped Christmas gift with a small mirror inside

What is this I hold in my hand? *(Christmas gift)* Of course, it is a Christmas present! Do you like to get Christmas presents? Of course you do — and so do I. I'm sure there will be lots of these under your Christmas tree on Christmas morning.

Where do you suppose the idea of giving gifts at Christmas time came from? Most people think they came from the three wise men who came to see Jesus when he was born. They brought him gold, frankincense, and myrrh, very expensive gifts. Why do we give gifts to one another at Christmas time? To show our family members and friends how much we think of them, how much we love them, right?

In a moment we are going to open this Christmas gift and find out what's in it. But, I'll tell you now it is something different. It represents a gift *you* can give to God. After all, it was God who gave us his Son as a gift at Christmas time, and we want to give something back to God for his precious gift, don't we?

Now, let's open this gift. I need a volunteer, someone who likes to open gifts. *(Everyone will volunteer, so you need to select one.)* All right, _____ will help us. Now, open it carefully and see what you find inside. *(Opens gift)* What is in the box, down at the bottom? Yes, a mirror. What do you see in the mirror? *(Myself)* Well, that represents the best gift you can give to God at Christmas time, or any other time. Yourself! There's nothing more important that you can give God than yourself!

So, remember, when you open your gifts this Christmas morning — they are gifts that are given to you because someone loves you. That is the same reason we give God the gift of ourselves at Christmas time, because we love him.

Second Sunday In Advent
A Dramatic Monologue
Suggested Scripture: Luke 2:1-7

The Innkeeper Speaks

Allow me to introduce myself. I am Jerash, the former keeper of the caravansary in Bethlehem. I am up in years now, but my memory still serves me well.

I want to tell you about a particular night a long time ago. Let's see, it would be something like 45 years ago now. I remember I turned away a young couple who were seeking shelter for the night. I remember the young woman was with child. The young man was hardly more than an apprentice. I have met many such couples, but this one stood out because, as I was told many years later, the son she bore turned out to be none other than God's *Messiah*, the Promised One of Israel! I still find that difficult to believe, but I am not prepared to say it is not true.

I remember this couple because they were so young and innocent. There was something about their countenance. It is hard to describe. It set them apart from the rank and file. The young woman appeared almost angelic. But I must continue with my story.

It was during one of the Roman taxations. That is very vivid in my mind. The city was crowded to overflowing. So many pilgrims. All desperately in search of shelter. I felt so sorry for the young woman because it appeared that she would go into labor at any moment.

Her husband told me they had been travelling five days and nights, all the way from Nazareth. "Nazareth?" I asked. "Isn't your young wife about to give birth to her child?" "Yes," he said, "that is why we must have shelter for the night!'' I had to tell him that every space was taken. Straw mats were everywhere on my property. Actually my heart went out to them. I remembered the sad look on the young husband's face as he turned to go away. Then, suddenly, it occurred to me. There was a stable not far from the inn, a natural limestone cave. I owned it, and only a few animals were there. At least it could give them some shelter. Get them out of the cold. ''Wait a moment,'' I called to him, ''I have a stable, a little way from the caravansary. It is the best I can offer.''

''We will take it!'' the young man said without hesitation.

He asked what it might cost, and I told him no one could charge for a stable. My wife took them to the cave; she wanted to make sure the young girl would be as comfortable as possible. She told me she volunteered to act as her midwife, and the couple gladly accepted. When the baby was born, that very evening, she stayed a couple of hours more, then came home. She said the young woman gave birth to a beautiful little boy.

I have heard some very interesting stories about the young child born in my stable that night. As I mentioned there are some who say he was God's promised Messiah. I ask myself, ''How can that be? God's Messiah born in a *stable?* That is not possible! He would be born under royal circumstances. He was to be a King. The King of the Jews!''

But, I heard the young man — *Jesus* — I think they called him, speak on several occasions. He would come to Bethlehem to visit relatives or friends. Everywhere he went crowds followed him. It was the same in Bethlehem. I did not know at first that it was he who was born in my stable. It was he, himself, who told me. He came by my inn on one of his visits and asked if he could see my stable. I thought that was rather an odd request. His mother had told him that was the place of his birth. I could not believe that this remarkable young man was the same one born that night in my stable. It was inspiring to listen to him. He was wise beyond his years. He captivated you with his kindness and his words of wisdom. I had never heard anyone speak quite like he spoke.

I heard the religious authorities in Jerusalem thought him to be a rabble-rouser. But I really think they were afraid of him. They were sure he was inciting a rebellion against them. I heard they had convinced one of his followers to betray him. Turn him over to the authorities. In no way could he cause a rebellion. He spoke of living *at peace* with God and our fellowmen. His message was one of love and compassion. He was incapable of harming anyone, and I am a good judge of character.

But, the word was that they trumped up some charges against him and took him before Pilate to have him *condemned to death!* Unbelievable! How could they hate such a good man? Why would they want him put to death?

But, they *had* him put to death by Roman crucifixion. One such as he should not have died such a horrible death. But, I heard of something even stranger happening to him. At one point I put little stock in it, but they say that a few days after his crucifixion he *rose from the dead!* No one has ever risen from the dead! That is quite unbelievable. Or so I would have argued at the time.

His followers, they call themselves "Followers of the Way," come here every year about this time. They say they want to see the place of his birth. Indeed, one of them purchased my stable for a considerable sum of money! He said it was to be preserved as a memorial to him. He — Nicodemus was his name — used to come here every year at this time, until he died a few years ago. He had a low stone wall built around the front of the cave . . . he said he wanted to mark the spot, for many would want to see it. He was right. There are more, many more, each year.

Nicodemus argued that Jesus of Nazareth *really was* God's Messiah, but not the kingly, conquering Messiah we all expected. Rather he was the *suffering* Messiah spoken of by Isaiah, and Micah, and also in the Book of Psalms. He recited the scriptures to me. I think he had committed them to memory. He said *I* automatically had a special relationship to him, because he was born on my property, in my stable.

I argued with Nicodemus. I could not accept a defeated Messiah. He was angry when I said "defeated." "No . . . not defeated," he said, "triumphant! He lives now at the right hand of God. I tell you, he *lives!* There is no one more alive than the risen Christ!"

He went on to say that we shall *all* live again! That death is nothing more than an illusion, a trick of the Adversary to convince us that we are mere mortals. No, because the Messiah lives, we, too, shall live, throughout the eternal ages to come! I wish I could believe him. For me it is too good to be true. I say I *wish* I could believe him. But that is not quite accurate. In my heart of hearts — somehow — I *do* believe him. My head says, "No, it cannot be," but my heart says, "Do not be so sure."

If it is true — and I pray that somehow it *is* true — then God has bestowed a special honor on me. In my humble stable he allowed the Messiah, the Savior of the world to be born!

For that honor I shall always be grateful, eternally grateful.

And I will *tell* him of my gratitude when I, too, come before his presence!

I can only say, "Lord, hasten the day!"

The First Christmas Tree

Object: Point to a Christmas tree that may be in the sanctuary, or bring a picture of a Christmas tree.

Do you know who first thought of the Christmas tree? No one knows for certain, but tradition tells us that Saint Boniface, a Catholic missionary in Germany in the eighth century, may have been the first one to pick the evergreen as a Christmas tree. He did so because the needles were always green, year round, and it represented the eternity of God to him. He used bright papers and ribbons to place on the tree because it represented the joy we have in knowing and following Christ.

Martin Luther, the founder of the Protestant Church, is supposed to be the first one who brought an evergreen tree inside his home and placed candles on it representing Christ the Light of the World.

Through the years people have decorated Christmas trees with Christian symbols, colorful bulbs, and later with little electric lights. Some string popcorn and place it on the tree.

It all represents the spirit of Christmas. The brightly decorated tree represents our joyful lives in Christ, and the lights represent Christ the Light of the World. Putting lights on our homes is a carry-over from decorating the tree.

I enjoy Christmas with its many colorful lights, and I enjoy the opportunity to give gifts to the ones we love. Is there anyone here who doesn't like Christmas?

27

Joseph Ponders

It is in the early hours of that first Christmas morn. In a natural cave just outside the city of Bethlehem is a young man, his even younger wife, and a newly-born child. The babe is nestled snugly in an animal-feeding trough deep inside the cave. Darkness still prevails, though the night has a thousand eyes with a myriad of stars. It will be several hours before dawn. The young man, Joseph, with the help of a midwife, has just helped in the delivery of his newborn son. The young woman, Mary, lies exhausted, leaning against the back wall of the cave on a straw mat. She is sleeping peacefully, as is the tiny infant. Joseph, however, is wide awake.

The midwife has left and returned to her family. Joseph's mind is keenly alert, though physically, he is exhausted. He would prefer to rest for a couple of hours, but his brain will not let him. So many events have indelibly impressed his senses this night. He closes his eyes and the drama is replayed once again. He ponders, to himself:

"Oh Lord, thank you. Thank you, for delivering the baby safely. I was afraid we would not make it to a place of shelter. I am so grateful that Mary can now find a few moments of rest. These last days have been so difficult for her. You know I would not have brought her on this long journey had it not been for the wagging tongues, the ones who looked at her out of the corners of their eyes. Her friends, even her own family, would not listen to her story — much less believe it. But, Lord, how can I blame them when I find it so hard to believe myself? In my dream, I still hear your voice, 'Joseph, son of David, do not fear to take Mary as your wife, for that which is conceived in her is of the Holy Spirit.' *The Holy Spirit!*

"I *know* Mary! She would not think of being untruthful! She is as baffled and confused as I. But the Babe is born. He lies here beside us. In my deepest being I *know* he is of divine origin, but who can comprehend the ways of the Almighty? *I* cannot understand it; how am I to make others understand? But, what I cannot understand I nevertheless accept, because you spoke to me. I *know* you spoke to me! And you spoke to Mary. She cannot explain it anymore than I, but neither of us would deny it.

"The night is so peaceful. My body is exhausted. But my mind is alert, alive, full of wonder. Miraculous wonder! Why? How did you choose us, Lord? Why *us?* We have *nothing* to offer your divine Son. He should have been born to royalty. At least to the wealthy. Those who could care properly for him. We have nothing, Lord, *nothing!* We are among the poorest of the poor. Surely you have miscalculated! *Alas!* Forgive me, Lord. Who am I to question the wisdom of the Almighty?

"You told me that Mary would bear a son, and a son it is, Lord, a beautiful, healthy son. You told us that we should name him Jesus, for he would save his people from their sins! The only one who can save our people, Lord, from their sins is the Anointed One of God! No! It cannot be! Such an honor could not be bestowed upon *us!*

"The scriptures, I remember, foretold that he would be born in Bethlehem. *Here!* In this very place! But, he was born here by *accident!* He should have been born in Nazareth where we live. But, Lord, you know of the census; I *had* to return to the city of my forefathers. Even under Mary's condition. I could not leave her! You know that.

"How could it be? That *all these circumstances* took place so that he would be born here? How are we to understand such workings of the Almighty?

"Listen! I hear footsteps! *Footsteps?* At this hour of the morning? Who would be wandering about at this hour? Lord, they have stopped. They are entering the cave! Are they here to harm us, Lord? They look like, they *are — shepherds!* What would bring them here at this hour? I can hardly make out their forms in this dim light. Who sent them? They evidently mean no harm. Why, they are *kneeling*, in front of the manger. Why do they not speak?

(In a half-whisper) *"You, there, what do you want? Why do you come here at this hour of the night?"*

(Voice of a young shepherd) "We have sought for a tiny babe, lying in a manger; God has led us to this place. This must be the child. And you, you must be its father. An angel appeared to us on the hillside, no more than an hour ago. And he said, 'This will be a sign for you: You will find a child wrapped in bands of cloth and lying in a manger. For unto you is born this day in the city of David a Savior, who is Christ the Lord! The Messiah!' My friend, is this indeed the Messiah? The Promised One of Israel? Have we found the child, or must we continue our search?"

"No, my friends. You have come to the right place. I cannot explain it anymore than you. But, yes, God has revealed it to us as well. This child, *his* child, is indeed the Promised One of Israel! Do not ask me how I know. I just know. It has been revealed to both my wife and me."

The shepherds gaze upon the child, and say nothing more. They kneel for a few moments, then leave, as silently as they came.

"Oh, my Lord! You have confirmed to us what we had dared not believe! You have sent the shepherds, to whom you also appeared! They have confirmed his birth, his identity, his *divinity!* How many others know of his birth, Lord?

"Mary does not know of the shepherds' visit. When she awakens, I will tell her. She will be thrilled to know that God has *confirmed* what he told us in a dream!

"It is silent once again. Such an unearthly silence. Such a God-like silence. I look upon this child. So fragile, so vulnerable. It is given to us to protect him, to raise him, to teach him. To *teach him?* How can we teach *him?* We have more need to be taught of him! But, I would vow this before you, Oh Lord. Before any harm will come to him they must first take my life! Mary and I, with your help, will share with him what we have. We can only teach him what we have been taught. Then you, Oh Lord, must supply the rest!

"Dawn! The first golden rays of light over the hillside! Surely this day will never be forgotten among men. As he grows, as he matures, we will understand more fully who he is and what his mission in life is to be. The shepherd said he was to be the Savior of the world! God grant that it may be so. Grant that the world may truly believe and be saved by him!

"Oh Lord, we humbly submit to your will. We shall never understand why you have chosen us, but we shall be forever grateful.

"If this beautiful child shall bring salvation to the world — to you, Oh Lord, be all the praise, honor, and glory! Amen."

The
Christmas Wreath

Object: A Christmas wreath (If there is one in the sanctuary, point to it. If not, bring a small one or a picture of one.)

You have all seen a Christmas wreath, I'm sure. See the one in the sanctuary *(point if there is one)* or (the one I hold in my hand). Tell me something about this wreath: What shape is it? Is it square? Is it round? Of course, it is round! Do you known *why* a Christmas wreath is round?

Let me tell you why: This wreath is round because it indicates it has no beginning and no end. Can you see where this wreath begins? Can you see where it ends? No. It is made that way to tell us of the eternity of God. God has no beginning and he has no end. He has been forever, and he will be forever.

Also, a wreath is made from an "evergreen" tree. It is generally made of pine needles. Pine needles are always green, year round. That is to show us that God does not change, he is always the same. That is why we choose Christmas trees to put in our homes. The Christmas tree is green, and its needles always stay the same color. A Christmas tree tells us that it, like God, is always the same.

Wreaths can be made very beautiful, with red ribbons, or pine cones, or even lights on them. But, the main thing about a wreath is that it is always green, telling us that God is always the same. And it is round to tell us that God is eternal.

Think about that the next time you see a Christmas wreath.

33

Fourth Sunday In Advent
A Dramatic Monologue
Suggested Scripture: Luke 1:26-35

Mary Remembers

I remember Bethlehem. How could I possibly forget?

My beloved Joseph and I made the 90-mile journey from Nazareth to Bethlehem in five days and nights. I argued with him that I should stay in Nazareth. It was too close to my delivery. He said he could not leave me there. It was too dangerous. He was right, of course. I could have been stoned to death for adultery. I saw the sly glances, the sneers on many faces. Some even accusing me of being unfaithful to Joseph.

How could I explain to them this strange, bewildering event? This miraculous birth? Would they believe me if I told them the angel Gabriel appeared to me that night — long ago — in my home in Nazareth? I can scarcely believe it myself. But, I can still hear the angel's voice: "Greetings, favored one! The Lord is with you." I was terrified. He stood in front of me in blazing white! His voice was so kind, his countenance so wondrous. He said to me, "Do not be afraid, Mary, for you have found favor with God. And now you will conceive in your womb and bear a son, and you will name him Jesus."

"How can this be?" I said. "Joseph and I have not yet consummated our marriage."

"The Holy Spirit will come upon you, and the power of the Most High will overshadow you; therefore the child to be born will be holy; he will be called the Son of God."

"The Son of God? This cannot be! I am not worthy. I am *the least* of all his servants!"

Lo! The angel was right! In a short time I realized I was with child! There was no other answer. It must be the Holy Spirit.

In about three months I visited my cousin, Elizabeth, for I had heard that she, too, was with child. Another miracle! She was well beyond the age of childbearing. Her husband, Zechariah, said it was indeed a miracle from God. When I saw Elizabeth, something within me confirmed the wonder of her pregnancy, as well as my own. My heart was filled to over-flowing!

I remember so well the night we arrived in Bethlehem. It was late, probably past midnight. I remember I was exhaust-ed, totally exhausted from the long trip. I barely remember Joseph talking to the keeper of the caravansary. I just remem-ber his coming back to me and saying there was no room in his inn. I was afraid that would be the case. Everyone needed a room for the night. The town was so crowded. Joseph, out of desperation, spoke again to the innkeeper. He told him I was near the time of my delivery. I remember the innkeeper coming over to us, and with compassion in his voice, he said: "I have no space left. I can only suggest one place — my sta-ble. It is clean there, and I can build a small fire. You will be away from the crowds. It is the best I can offer."

"We will take it!" Joseph said. "But, I fear our child may be born this very night! Do you have any hot water and some clean cloths? I would be willing to pay you for them."

"Of course we have. My wife will see that you get them. But, now let us get to the stable and make your wife as com-fortable as possible."

"I am in your eternal debt, sir. I will never forget your kindness," Joseph replied.

I knew that I would give birth that night. The journey was almost more than I could bear.

Through the night I was in constant labor pain, mixed with feelings of apprehension, exhaustion, fear, but also trust. My mind went through every emotion. My one overwhelming desire was to give my child a healthy birth.

If the angel was correct, if this indeed was to be the Son of God, he should not be born under these circumstances! I should at least be at home in Nazareth, in the warmth and security of our home. My mother would be there to tell me what to do, to take charge of the birth. The innkeeper's wife agreed to act as midwife. Thank God for that. But I still felt so alone, so inexperienced, so frightened!

My good Joseph. He arranged for everything. He tried so hard. It is still so vivid in my mind. The cave was warm and cozy. A good fire was going. The midwife was by my side. Joseph had finally fallen asleep, totally exhausted.

Toward morning I gave birth to my firstborn. The joy of seeing my newborn son, holding him in my arms, erased all the pain, all the anxiety. As the babe lay cozy in my arms, I finally slept.

When I awoke Joseph told me that we had some visitors, some shepherds from a nearby hillside. They had had an angelic visitation, and the angel announced to them that they would find the baby, God's Messiah, the Promised One of Israel, in Bethlehem, in a stable. I was so relieved that some others had confirmed his birth. God again confirmed to both Joseph and me what we almost dared not believe.

God has confirmed his actions over and over again in my life, and the life of my Son. I know beyond a shadow of a doubt that he is the Son of God, the Savior of the world. If I ever had cause to doubt, all that has been removed. God has affirmed his every action, over and over again.

How my mind is flooded with memories of him: How he grew, his first steps, his first words, his teething. And something more, his nobility. Yes, his nobility. He was no ordinary child, even from the beginning. He was mature beyond his years. As a young child, his teachers, the rabbis in the synagogue, all recognized his unusual, deeply spiritual mind. They confessed they had reached the stage where his answers were more profound than theirs! How could one so young be so wise, so beyond his years?

My other four sons and two daughters — I guess I should call them my "natural" children — never could understand him. When my beloved Joseph died at such an early age, Jesus, as the eldest, took charge of the household. Perhaps that is the reason his brothers and sisters resented him. But he *was* different from them! I must confess that often times I did not understand him, all he said, all he did. But I never had any doubts about his relationship with God.

I remember the time we thought we had lost him after the visit to Jerusalem for his Bar-Mitzvah. We hurried back to the city, went to the temple area and found him disputing with the lawyers. He wondered why we were looking for him! "Did you not know that I must be about my Father's business?" he said. Neither his father nor I understood what he meant. *He* was not all that concerned, and wondered why we should be.

I remember very well the time his brothers and sisters insisted I go with them when he was teaching in one of the nearby homes. They were convinced he was beside himself. He was saying such strange things. People were talking. The only decent thing to do was to bring him home and keep him away from the public. I agreed to go, but only because of their insistence. He did not even come out to see us when he was told we were outside. He sent word to us: "Who is my mother, my brother, my sister? Those who do the will of God, they are my mother and my brethren." I must confess I felt hurt. But I should have recognized once again that he was not *my* son. He belonged to God, to those who needed him.

I won't go into the last days of his life. It is too painful for me to recall. He would never have led an insurrection. He was not a man of violence. He would not harm a hair of any individual. It was the Jewish authorities who condemned him. Pilate merely acquiesced to their wishes.

Oh, why didn't they recognize that he had the answer to peace, *real* peace! He brought words directly from God, words that would liberate the world from evil, and ultimate destruction! But, his words only served to infuriate the authorities, and they insisted on his death.

I do not speak of him as *my* son anymore. He was never truly mine. We, my sons and daughters, knelt with those in the upper room on the day of Pentecost, awaiting the baptism of the Holy Spirit. I knelt in homage to him who was now, not so much my son, as my Lord. I saw him crucified. But I also saw him in his resurrected body! I know now, more than I have ever known before, that he truly was — is — the Son of God!

But, I shall always treasure the fact that he was born to me, that he was *my* son, my beloved son, if even for a brief time.

On this eve of his birth, I remember — yes — *I remember so well!*

Who Is
Santa Claus?

Object: Picture of Santa Claus

Many years ago there was a first Santa Claus. It was really a young Russian bishop named Nicolas who lived during the fourth century in Turkey. He was elected a bishop when still a boy. He was a very kind person and used to give gifts to the poor, not only at Christmas time, but throughout the year.

When he died many years later he had become famous for his generosity and others began to copy his habit of giving gifts to the poor and to their friends and family. Eventually he became associated with Christmas, a time when God gave the finest gift of all to the world, his Son, and the three wise men gave gifts to Jesus at his birth.

His name was changed to Santa Claus when the Dutch settlers first came to America (in New York City). The Dutch called him Sant Nikelaas, but the children soon shortened it to Santa Claus.

Many stories have been written about Santa Claus, especially by the Americans, and today he is a somewhat different person than the original Saint Nicolas. Our current picture of Santa Claus comes from a theologian who was writing a poem to his children one Christmas Eve, and the poem is called " 'Twas the Night Before Christmas.'' In it he describes a little old man dressed in red, with a long white beard, and a sleigh with eight tiny reindeer.

Whether we think of a little, old man in a red suit and long beard, or a Saint Nicolas who lived back in the fourth century, the spirit of Christmas still lives, as does the spirit of sharing and giving.

Jesus Reflects

Jesus of Nazareth speaks: This is the 33rd year since my birth, and in my travels I have come to Bethlehem several times. But, this is the first time I have been here on the night of my birth. I felt drawn here this year, for somehow I instinctively feel I will be unable to visit it again. I know those who oppose me seek to silence me, and I fear before long they may succeed.

But, I did not come here to reflect on such thoughts. I have come to see once again the place where my mother brought me into the world. Over the years it seems it has changed little, if at all. There is a new owner of the caravansary, and the cave. He, too, keeps his animals here.

My mother has related the story to me many times: The shepherds on the hillside, the angelic announcement, their hurried trip into Bethlehem and finally locating this cave, my mother and father's anguish in trying to find a place to stay, the kindness of the innkeeper to give us this cave, and his wife offering to be a midwife to Mary. A bit later, when we were able to stay with some friends in a home in the city, the *visit of the magi!* I have longed to find and speak to one of them, but unfortunately our paths have never crossed.

I look at this cave, hewn by nature out of the hillside. A humble birthplace many would say. But, while it was rough-hewn, it was clean and warm, and my mother says it was not the most uncomfortable place to give birth to a baby. She has told me of the circumstances of my birth, that my beloved father, Joseph, was not my real father. I have known since

43

my early teens that I was different from other children. God has spoken to me, I would have to say, directly, every day of my adult life, and even before that. I now realize that I was with him before my birth in the heaven of heavens, and that I indeed *volunteered* for my mission on earth.

My mother has told me of the shame she bore by being with child during her engagement to Joseph. People could not accept the fact that she was of child of the Holy Spirit. There were those who wanted to stone her for her unfaithfulness. They called her an adulteress. I am so proud of my mother and father's obedience to God! How easy it would have been to refuse God's plan and live a simple life in Nazareth!

I cannot explain to you my nature; it is still a mystery to me. I only know that God directs my life, and I am content to follow his direction each day. I would go so far as to say that my Father and I are *one*, certainly in spirit!

I do not look upon my birth as particularly miraculous. In my view all births are miraculous! God is the creator of human life, and apart from him none would exist. He has as well created *my* life, only in a somewhat different manner.

If man could only recognize it — life truly is more *divine* than human! God has poured so much of his creative genius into man, and has made men and women just a little lower than himself. No other creature has been granted that privilege. Man's potential, if only he could recognize it, is astonishing! All of heaven awaits him! If only my brethren among the Hebrews could recognize that life does not end with the grave! The grave is nothing more than a door through which we must pass in our further spiritual development.

One of the frustrations — true frustrations — of my mission has been the sobering recognition that few people are aware of their true, spiritual potential! So many are caught up solely in the day-to-day struggle for survival. Many have become captive to their fleshly desires. Many others have expended all their energy upon self-gratification, using any means to achieve their selfish desires. And it is all so temporal, so transitory! I have found it almost impossible to open their eyes to their true potential. I know it is a frustration for *God, himself,* who finds it difficult to comprehend the very being he has created!

I do not say that none have responded. Thank God many have come to a knowledge of their true potential, and have elected to give their lives completely to God. But, strictly speaking, they are few among the many.

I have sometimes been asked: "When did you first recognize your unique gifts?" I think I was around the age of ten. I recall our family dog having broken his leg, and he limped around our home for several days. I felt so sorry for him. Why couldn't someone help him? Almost by chance I put my hand on his leg and prayed that it would be healed. It was healed at that moment! But, the dog turned around and snarled at me! He could not understand what had happened, and he was frightened. I, too, was startled and frightened! How was I able to do that, by simply touching and praying for him?

I would soon learn that such powers had indeed been granted to me, and I still find it rather remarkable. God would grant me the privilege of healing countless individuals, and more important, seeing them give God the credit for their healing. More often than not their spirits were healed at the same time. Such was the purpose of healing — that the spirit would be healed in the process.

I have been asked many times if I am God's Messiah. I am *not* the Messiah the multitudes yearn for: the kingly, conquering Messiah; he who would put down the enemies of our people; he who would establish righteousness in the world by divine fiat; he who would usher in a veritable paradise on earth where no evil would exist. God revealed to me that I had the gifts to play that role, but it was not to be. It would in no way *change man's heart!* Furthermore, it would reduce man to nothing more than a puppet with God as the manipulator. It would not cause man to give his heart to God in loving obedience and service. Man is by deliberate design a creature of *choice!* He is granted the *awesome responsibility* of choice! He must *willingly* give his love and obedience to God, or it is worthless.

I was given the opportunity to prove my unique powers a number of times in my ministry. When my disciples and I fed the multitudes upon the hillside — some 5,000, not including the women and children — and later feeding 4,000, all that resulted from it was their return the next day to be fed! No lives were changed.

I was given the power to raise the dead, and did so on several occasions — including my dear friend, Lazarus — but it resulted in few if any giving their lives to God. God has revealed to me that I could eliminate hunger, and even death. Such powers are at my disposal. But, what would it really accomplish in the final analysis?

No, the only answer to humankind's salvation, is for God to first show man how much *he* loves *him,* and allow man to freely respond to such love or, should he so choose, reject it. It is as simple — and as profound — as that. And God has revealed to me the terrible price that must be paid for the proof of such love. All genuine love demands sacrifice, and the greater the love the greater the sacrifice.

I know my destiny is the cross. I have known it for some time. Isaiah decreed it many years ago: "Like a lamb that is led to the slaughter." Humanly speaking, of course, I dread such an experience, but, knowing it is possibly the only way man will be convinced of God's love, I accept it.

Would you believe that God (and I) *longed for* people to respond to his message of love? My ministry was essentially a ministry of love: of healing, of forgiveness, of reconciliation. But, for the most part it has been rejected. If men do not respond to the message of the cross they are left to their own designs and judgment. What more can God do?

For now, however, I wish to soak up the peacefulness of this night. I lay here on my back and gaze up into the heavens. The jeweled sky! The marvel of the world and this vast universe! The handiwork of God! The same God who would give to, as well as seek, the love of his creatures, believing that such love would freely be reciprocated. How sad that it often is not!

46

I rejoice for those who have come to a knowledge of the truth! I am convinced that countless others will come to that knowledge, through the witness of those who have found it. I shall go obediently to my death. But, in a larger sense I shall go to *life* once again with God, my Father. God has assured me that resurrection shall follow my death. Resurrection will in countless ways confirm my mission.

But, for now, I shall simply lay here and rejoice in God, my Father, and commune with him once again, under this marvelous canopy of stars in the quietness and peacefulness of this night.

Jesus, The
Light Of The World

Object: A candle

(Hold the candle in your hand and refer to it from time to time. You may wish to light it at one point in the story, perhaps when you speak of Jesus as the Light of the World.)

Today is Christmas Sunday. Did you know that the first Christmas trees had candles on them instead of small light bulbs? We believe it was Martin Luther, the founder of the Protestant Church, who first put candles on a Christmas tree that he brought into his home. The candle was to represent Jesus.

Let's think about Jesus as the Light of the World this morning. That's what Jesus said about himself, "I am the Light of the world."

Tell me what you know about light. If a candle glows in a dark room does it help us to see? *(Yes)* Light also helps things to grow, like the flowers that grow in the sunlight. The heat from the light of a fire keeps us warm. Light makes it possible for us to work and play at night when it would ordinarily be dark. We wouldn't have television without light coming from the screen on your television set. Light has many purposes, and it is certainly a gift from God.

Light also reminds us of joy. Greyness or darkness is associated with sadness. Light is also a symbol of life, just as darkness is a symbol of death. Did you know there would be no colors unless we had light? There are no colors in complete darkness.

Many of the qualities of light help us to understand what Jesus meant when he said he was the Light of the World. Jesus brightens our lives and makes us glad to be alive. He helps us to grow, just like the sunlight helps the flowers to grow. We feel warm and secure in his presence. We are not afraid when he is near us. He makes our lives alive, colorful, meaningful, and gives us a purpose for living.

We celebrate Christmas because Jesus, as the Light of the World, came to us in the form of a little baby many years ago. When you see the lights on your Christmas tree, think of Jesus, the Light of the World.

You will not walk in darkness if Jesus is with you.

Sunday After Christmas
A Dramatic Monologue
Suggested Scripture: Luke 2:25-35

Simeon Recalls

My name is Simeon. I am advanced in years, but the Lord revealed to me that before I die I would see God's Anointed One, the Messiah. I know we have waited centuries for him to come, but I tell you — *he has come!* I saw him, I held him — as an infant — in my arms. When his parents came to the temple the other day with this precious child the Lord revealed to me that he was indeed the Messiah, the Promised One of God!

I have prayed all my adult life that I would be able to see him, should he come in my lifetime. It is beyond my comprehension that the Lord would send him now, after all these years! But God has confirmed to me that the one I held in my arms, for a brief moment, was indeed the promised Deliverer!

And God has revealed much more to me about this Promised One. This revelation has come through prayer. I *did not want* to believe what God has revealed to me through earnest prayer! I wanted to believe that he is the One who will restore Israel to its former glory, as in the days of King David. I wanted to believe that peace would come to the entire world, with his coming. I wanted to believe that our enemies would be put down, that righteousness would reign, that hunger, disease, pestilence would be done away with.

But, God has revealed to me another role for the Messiah. A *suffering* Messiah! He has pointed me to the Prophet Isaiah and his writings on the One who would suffer to bring about salvation to the world. Oh, Lord, have we not seen enough suffering? That has been the history of our people! Even now we are a conquered people, living under the yoke of Rome. Must there always be suffering? Why, why must your Messiah also suffer?

But, again God reminded me of the words of the Prophet Isaiah: "Yet it was the will of the Lord to crush him with pain. When you make his life an offering for sin, he shall see his offspring, and shall prolong his days; through him the will of the Lord shall prosper. Out of his anguish he shall see light; he shall find satisfaction through his knowledge. The righteous one, my servant, shall make many righteous; and he shall bear their iniquities. Therefore I will divide the spoil with the strong; because he poured out himself to death, and was numbered with the transgressors; yet he bore the sin of many, and made intercession for the transgressors." Yes, I have committed much of Isaiah to memory.

In his infinite wisdom God has revealed to me that man is not fit to reign with God in a righteous society, *for man is not righteous!* Our own people, the Israelites, are not qualified to rule with God's Messiah! They must themselves become righteous! They *must* repent of their sin and commit their lives to him.

No, God's Messiah is destined to be, as Isaiah has said, "like a lamb that is led to the slaughter ... stricken for the transgression of my people."

I told this to his parents, but I am sure they did not understand what I was saying. My words to them: "This child is destined for the falling and the rising of many in Israel, and to be a sign that will be opposed." I told his mother: "A sword will pierce your own soul too." She seemed saddened, and bewildered, as did her husband. But, they must know the truth! They must not harbor the delusions I had about the Conquering Messiah! They cannot understand his life, and especially his death, if they do.

Why are men so calloused of heart? Why will they not recognize God's true nature and what he desires of his people?

I should have known! Our people have time and again stoned the prophets sent to them!

But, Anna, my good friend who comes to the temple every day to pray, she, too, has recognized that Israel must be *redeemed* before it can rule with God's Messiah.

For myself, I still delight in holding that precious infant and knowing that he will fulfill God's will and purpose for humanity — even though it be the path of suffering. Through him God will call a righteous people, those worthy of dwelling with him both here and hereafter.

I told my Lord after holding the child: "Master, now you are dismissing your servant in peace, according to your word; for my eyes have seen your salvation."

I shall soon depart this world. I have no regrets. God has also revealed to me that the end is really the beginning! Life continues beyond this "veil of tears."

What more can we ask?

But, while I have breath, I shall pray for this young child and his divine mission. I have no fear that he will fail, but I know that he will need the prayers of God's people for his day-to-day struggle. Even under divine command there is pain.

I cannot believe that God's plan will suffer defeat. In his great wisdom he has decreed this means for man's salvation, and I am confident God will achieve his goal.

Following the night there is always the promise of the glorious dawn!

Praying Hands

Object: Albrecht Durer's "Praying Hands" (either a small statue of "Praying Hands" or a picture)

Our minister will talk this morning about Simeon, one of the people who knew Jesus as a baby. Simeon was also one who prayed a great deal, and it was through prayer that Simeon found out that Jesus was the Son of God and the Savior of the world.

But I want to talk this morning about another man who prayed a great deal, and was honored for his prayers by his friend drawing a picture of his hands folded in prayer.

I have in my hands a famous statue *(picture)* called "Praying Hands." It is really a copy of a famous picture painted by Albrecht Durer who lived over 500 years ago in Germany. He painted many other pictures but this is his most famous.

Albrecht was a part of a large family which was very poor, so Albrecht started to work at a very early age. He wanted more than anything else to be an artist, but there was no time or money. When he became a young adult he convinced his parents that he could make a living as an artist, but he would have to leave home and go to one of the large cities. His parents said he should go.

He went into a large city and studied under a famous artist for a short time, but what little money he had ran out and he had to get any work he could, just to stay alive. He met another man, somewhat older than he, who also wanted to be an artist and they decided to room together to save expenses.

For a time they both worked at any job they could find, but neither was getting anywhere as an artist.

Finally the older man suggested that he work for both of them while Durer tried to find work as an artist. When Durer became a successful artist they would both quit work and concentrate on their art. After several years Durer did become successful as an artist, and told his friend that he could now take up his work as an artist, for he (Durer) made enough for both of them to live. But his older friend had found that his fingers had become too sore (from the hard work he had been doing to make a living). He was unable to paint anymore, so he had to give up his desire to become an artist.

One day when Durer returned home he thought he heard the voice of his friend in prayer in another room. He quietly opened the door and saw him praying at a table with his hands folded in prayer, like this *(show the picture or the statue again)*. Durer said he would give the world a picture of those gnarled and calloused hands out of gratitude for his friend's work through the years. So, he painted the famous painting that we see here today.

We can use our hands for many things. We may not all be talented like an artist, but we can use our hands for many other things. A carpenter must use his hands to work. So must a plumber, an electrician, a grocery clerk, a person who works at a desk. There are few things you *can* do without your hands. Use your hands to help others as well as yourself, and God will richly reward you for it. Remember Jesus said, "Inasmuch as you did it unto one of the least of these my brethren, you did it unto me."

Epiphany Sunday
A Dramatic Monologue
Suggested Scripture: Matthew 2:1-12

Melchior Reminisces

My name is Melchior. I am one of the astrologers that came to Bethlehem several years ago in search of the new-born King of Israel.

I am from Persia, and am in the court of the King of Persia. We, as magi, study the stars and are convinced they foretell the destiny of individuals and nations. My brethren and I are deeply religious, also, and believe that the Great God of the universe directs all things in both nations and individuals. Our basic religion is Zoroastrianism, founded by Zarathustra, many years ago. It is a monotheistic religion much like the Judean religion of the Hebrews. We, too, subscribe to the belief that the contest between good and evil is everywhere visible in our world. We honor the scriptures of Israel and admire the teachings of Moses and the prophets. We recognize that they expect their long-awaited Messiah and have prayed for centuries for him to come. We, too, are greatly interested in this Messiah for it is our belief as well that he will rule the world as God's special representative.

You can imagine our delight when we saw the convergence of several planets in the east, what is now called the Star of Bethlehem! We were sure, my brethren and I, that an unusual birth had taken place and were determined to journey to that star and discover who that personage might be. We were quite convinced it was the Messiah, the King of Israel, but we wanted to be certain.

We discussed this with the King of Persia and he agreed that we should make the trip. It would be long and arduous, many, many miles across the Syrian Desert, but we were determined to go. The king suggested we take with us gifts suitable for a king: gold, frankincense and myrrh. He told us also to visit King Herod and offer him our congratulations on the birth of the new monarch.

We prepared ourselves for the long journey. We took an ample supply of food and drink, tents, clothing and the gifts. Our camels were of the best breed for the long journey. We knew that we would not arrive in time for the Messiah's birth, but we hoped to be able to see him and present him our gifts.

We, too, knew that the birth of the King of Israel was to take place in Bethlehem. This we had learned from the Hebrew scriptures. Our calculations told us that the special star was somewhere over the city of Bethlehem.

After many days and nights (I don't think any of us made count) we arrived in Jerusalem and sought an audience with King Herod. We inquired of him where the young King may be, and he seemed quite surprised that a King had been born! He questioned us for some time and said that we should tell him when we found him, for he, too, wanted to come and pay homage to him. He appeared somewhat suspicious and uneasy. We said that we would tell him when and if we found the child, thinking that he would, indeed, want to pay homage to such an important personage. But, we were warned in a dream that we should not inform King Herod, and should seek an alternate route home, bypassing King Herod. In the dream, which incidentally was my own, I was told that Herod might want to take the life of the young child since he was very jealous of his throne.

We went our way to Bethlehem and, sure enough, the Star of Bethlehem shone directly over the city! We were now sure that the Kingly Messiah had been born, and we must see him! We inquired of several, and finally found one individual who seemed to know something of his whereabouts. We were told that he was born in a cave! A stable for horses and cows!

We could not comprehend this. We went to the caravansary on the outskirts of Bethlehem (where we were told he was born) and talked at some length to the owner, a man by the name of Jerash. He told us that a baby had been born in his stable several days ago, and it was his understanding that the young couple and baby were staying with some friends in a home in Bethlehem. He did not know exactly where it was, but told us of one in Bethlehem who should know. After some inquiry we were told of a home in which the King of Israel dwelt! We went immediately and found him! His mother, Mary, and father, Joseph, were quite surprised to see us — all the way from Persia!

We looked at the beautiful child in his crib and sank to our knees in gratitude to the Almighty for enabling us to find him. When we presented our gifts to his parents they received them with humble gratitude. We stayed but a short time. But we heard from his father that he, too, had a dream in which he was warned to flee to Egypt, for Herod was determined to destroy the child! How could that be? Did not Herod know that God would protect this special child whose birth was proclaimed by the stars? Mary and Joseph planned to leave the next day, and we urged them to do so. I told them of the dream I had had, also, and we did not plan to return to Jerusalem.

On our long journey home, my friends and I discussed the fascinating circumstances surrounding the birth of the Kingly child. We could not fathom King Herod and his desire to destroy the infant, but word reached us several months after we had returned that he had sent his soldiers to Bethlehem and had destroyed all the male infants two years of age and under! Surely that could not be! But, we had received the word on good authority.

But, he had not destroyed the young King! For that we were most grateful.

Who knows what lies in the future for the young King? He already has his enemies! But, I believe his reign will be blessed by the Almighty, and he will bring peace and justice to this world of ours. I look forward with eager anticipation to his reign, should God grant that I live that long. Surely the world will be a much better place for all of us!

I remember the words of the Prophet Isaiah who proclaimed the coming of this marvelous King: "For to us a child is born, to us a son is given, and the government shall be upon his shoulder. And his name will be called Wonderful Counselor, Mighty God, Everlasting Father, Prince of Peace!"

God grant that I shall see his reign in my lifetime!

A Brand New Page

Object: A blank piece of paper and a pencil with an eraser

We are still at the beginning of a New Year and many people like to think in terms of getting a fresh start. In a sense, starting over again.

Something like a blank sheet of paper, such as I hold in my hand this morning. There is nothing written on this paper. Let's say we haven't done anything in the New Year yet. Most of us would like to put down some very good things we do this year — such as coming to Sunday school and church each Sunday, obeying our parents, making good grades in school, being nice to other people. As we do all of them they will be written down in the New Year.

But, when we do something wrong, that is written down, also. Now, how do we get rid of the things we do wrong? We can pray and ask God for forgiveness. We can also ask a friend or our parents for their forgiveness if we have done something wrong to them. Let the forgiveness we ask for be like this pencil's eraser. See, if I have something wrong written on my paper, I can ask God, through prayer, to forgive it. And he will erase it from the paper! *(Erase something you have written on the paper.)* It's as if it didn't happen at all, though of course we know it did.

Try to make good entries on your sheet of paper this year by doing lots of good things. But, remember when you do something wrong God still has an eraser, called forgiveness. He can make the sheet white again. And at the same time he asks us to try not to do it again. Have a good New Year!